Jr. Graphic Biographies™

HARRIET TUBMAN
and the Underground Railroad

Dan Abnett

PowerKiDS
press
New York

Published in 2007 by The Rosen Publishing Group, Inc.
29 East 21st Street, New York, NY 10010

First Edition

Editors: Joanne Randolph and Nel Yomtov
Book Design: Julio Gil
Illustrations: Q2A

Library of Congress Cataloging-in-Publication Data

Abnett, Dan.
  Harriet Tubman and the Underground Railroad / Dan Abnett.— 1st ed.
     p. cm. — (Jr. graphic biographies)
  Includes index.
  ISBN (10) 1-4042-3393-8 (13) 978-1-4042-3393-5 (lib. bdg.) —
ISBN (10) 1-4042-2146-8 (13) 978-1-4042-2146-8 (pbk.)
  1. Tubman, Harriet, 1820?–1913—Juvenile literature. 2. Slaves—United States—Biography—Juvenile literature. 3. African American women—Biography—Juvenile literature. 4. Underground railroad—Juvenile literature. I. Title. II. Series.

E444.T82A26 2007
973.7'115092—dc22

                                                                    2005037162

Manufactured in the United States of America

CONTENTS

MAIN CHARACTERS

Harriet Tubman (c. 1822–1913) was born into slavery. When she was about 27 years old, she escaped. Tubman helped about 300 slaves leave the South to find freedom in places throughout North America. She later worked for the Union army during the **Civil War**. Harriet Tubman also fought for women's rights and the rights of the poor.

William Still (1821–1902) was the son of ex-slaves. He was called the Father of the **Underground Railroad**. Still helped about 60 slaves a month escape to freedom. He kept careful records about each slave he helped free. In a book he wrote, Still claimed that he helped 649 slaves escape to freedom on the Underground Railroad.

Thomas Garrett (1789–1871) was an **abolitionist** who worked on the Underground Railroad in Delaware. Garrett worked with Tubman many times to free slaves. He claimed that he helped free 2,500 slaves.

HARRIET TUBMAN AND
THE UNDERGROUND RAILROAD

IN THE EIGHTEENTH AND NINETEENTH CENTURIES, SLAVERY WAS VERY COMMON IN THE SOUTHERN PART OF THE UNITED STATES.

SLAVES WERE BLACK PEOPLE WHO WERE **CAPTURED** IN AFRICA AND THEN BROUGHT TO AMERICA AND SOLD.

MOST SLAVES WORKED ON **PLANTATIONS**. SLAVES WERE THE PROPERTY OF THEIR MASTERS.

SLAVE CHILDREN DID NOT GO TO SCHOOL. THEY HAD TO WORK HARD AT A VERY YOUNG AGE.

ARAMINTA ROSS WAS BORN A SLAVE IN MARYLAND, IN 1822. WHEN SHE WAS ABOUT SIX, SHE BEGAN WORKING FOR A **WEAVER**.

ARAMINTA WAS OFTEN TREATED VERY BADLY.

ARAMINTA BECAME VERY ILL WITH THE MEASLES.

WHEN SHE FELT BETTER, ARAMINTA WENT TO WORK AS A HOUSEKEEPER AND BABYSITTER.

AT 11, ARAMINTA CHANGED HER NAME TO HARRIET, WHICH WAS HER MOTHER'S NAME.

AT 12, HARRIET SAW AN **OVERSEER** TRYING TO TIE UP A YOUNG SLAVE. HARRIET WAS AFRAID.

THE SLAVE BROKE FREE AND STARTED TO RUN. THE OVERSEER THREW AN IRON WEIGHT AT HIM BUT HIT HARRIET INSTEAD. HARRIET WAS BADLY HURT.

AROUND 1844, HARRIET MARRIED A FREE MAN NAMED JOHN TUBMAN.

ONE DAY WE WILL TRAVEL NORTH, WHERE WE CAN BE FREE FROM SLAVERY.

I AM A FREE MAN ALREADY. I AM HAPPY HERE.

OTHER SLAVES HAVE ESCAPED. MAYBE I CAN, TOO.

WHERE WOULD YOU GO, HARRIET?

IN 1849, HARRIET TUBMAN'S OWNER, EDWARD BRODESS, DIED. HE LEFT MRS. BRODESS WITH LARGE **DEBTS**.

MRS. BRODESS WOULD HAVE TO SELL HER SLAVES TO PAY BACK THE MONEY SHE OWED.

TUBMAN DECIDED TO RUN AWAY.

SHE WENT TO THE HOME OF SOMEONE WHO COULD HELP HER.

WHY DO YOU HELP SLAVES?

SLAVERY IS WRONG. PEOPLE SHOULD NOT OWN PEOPLE OR TREAT THEM BADLY.

TUBMAN SECRETLY LEFT MARYLAND. SHE HID UNDER SOME SACKS IN A WAGON SO THAT SHE WOULD NOT BE SEEN.

HARRIET TUBMAN WAS FINALLY FREE. SHE WORKED HARD TO EARN MONEY TO HELP OTHER SLAVES.

TUBMAN MET WILLIAM STILL IN PHILADELPHIA. HE HELPED SLAVES ESCAPE FROM THE SOUTH.

STILL TOLD HER THE STORY OF ONE SLAVE WHOM HE HELPED.

HENRY BROWN WANTED SO MUCH TO BE FREE, HARRIET. HE MAILED HIMSELF TO ME IN A WOODEN BOX!

HENRY'S STORY FILLS ME WITH HOPE.

HARRIET, WE WANT YOU TO BECOME A "CONDUCTOR" ON THE UNDERGROUND RAILROAD.

STILL EXPLAINED THAT HELPING SLAVES ESCAPE WOULD NOT BE EASY. A NEW LAW, CALLED THE **FUGITIVE** SLAVE ACT, SAID SLAVES COULD BE CAUGHT ANYWHERE IN THE COUNTRY AND RETURNED TO THEIR OWNERS.

TUBMAN WAS NOT AFRAID. SHE LEARNED THE **ROUTES** OF THE UNDERGROUND RAILROAD. SHE TOOK AN **OATH** OF SILENCE.

HOLY BIBLE

IN 1850, TUBMAN LEARNED THAT HER NIECE AND HER NIECE'S TWO CHILDREN WERE GOING TO BE SOLD IN CAMBRIDGE, MARYLAND.

HARRIET IS FREE. SHE WILL HELP US. WE MUST NOT BE AFRAID.

TUBMAN WENT TO HELP HER FAMILY ESCAPE TO FREEDOM.

THE FAMILY TRAVELED ACROSS PENNSYLVANIA. THEY VISITED SEVERAL SAFE HOUSES ON THEIR JOURNEY.

SLAVES WERE SAFEST WHEN THEY TRAVELED AT NIGHT AND KEPT AWAY FROM BUSY PLACES.

WHEN THEY ARRIVED IN THE FREE STATES OF THE NORTH, THE SLAVES COULD STILL BE CAUGHT AND RETURNED TO THEIR OWNERS.

AFTER HER FIRST SUCCESSFUL **MISSION**, HARRIET TUBMAN CONTINUED TO MAKE JOURNEYS TO THE SOUTH TO **RESCUE** SLAVES.

IT WAS A HARD JOURNEY. THE SLAVES COULD BE CAPTURED OR KILLED.

SLAVES CONTINUED TO ESCAPE THE SOUTH ANYWAY.

WE'LL CROSS THE RIVER AND GET TO THOMAS GARRETT'S HOUSE IN DELAWARE. HE'S HELPED MORE SLAVES THAN ANYONE ELSE I KNOW.

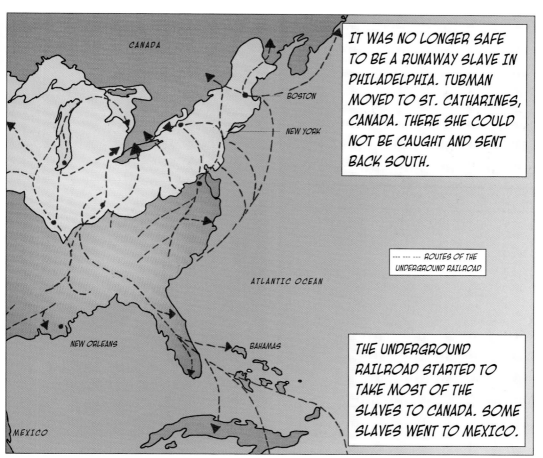

IT WAS NO LONGER SAFE TO BE A RUNAWAY SLAVE IN PHILADELPHIA. TUBMAN MOVED TO ST. CATHARINES, CANADA. THERE SHE COULD NOT BE CAUGHT AND SENT BACK SOUTH.

--- --- --- ROUTES OF THE UNDERGROUND RAILROAD

THE UNDERGROUND RAILROAD STARTED TO TAKE MOST OF THE SLAVES TO CANADA. SOME SLAVES WENT TO MEXICO.

ON ONE ROUTE FROM NEW YORK STATE TO CANADA, SLAVES HAD TO CROSS AN UNSAFE BRIDGE NEAR THE NIAGARA FALLS.

IN 1851, HARRIET TUBMAN RETURNED TO MARYLAND.

WHAT ARE YOU DOING HERE?

YOU ARE MY HUSBAND, JOHN. I HAVE COME TO TAKE YOU HOME.

THIS IS MY HOME, HARRIET. I WILL NOT COME WITH YOU.

I HAVE A NEW WIFE NOW.

YOU HAVE **BETRAYED** ME AND OUR PEOPLE. GOOD-BYE, JOHN.

TUBMAN TRAVELED BACK NORTH. SHE STOPPED AT THOMAS GARRETT'S HOUSE.

THERE ARE MANY PEOPLE HERE WHO NEED TO BE LED TO SAFETY.

I'LL HELP THEM, THOMAS.

WE'RE GOING TO GET CAUGHT. I WANT TO GO BACK!

NO ONE'S GOING BACK. YOU HAVE NO CHOICE. MOVE . . . OR DIE!

THE SLAVES HARRIET TUBMAN LED TO SAFETY WERE OFTEN SCARED. THE JOURNEY FROM THE SOUTH TO CANADA WAS LONG AND HARD. TUBMAN DID WHAT SHE HAD TO DO TO MAKE SURE THEY MADE IT TO FREEDOM.

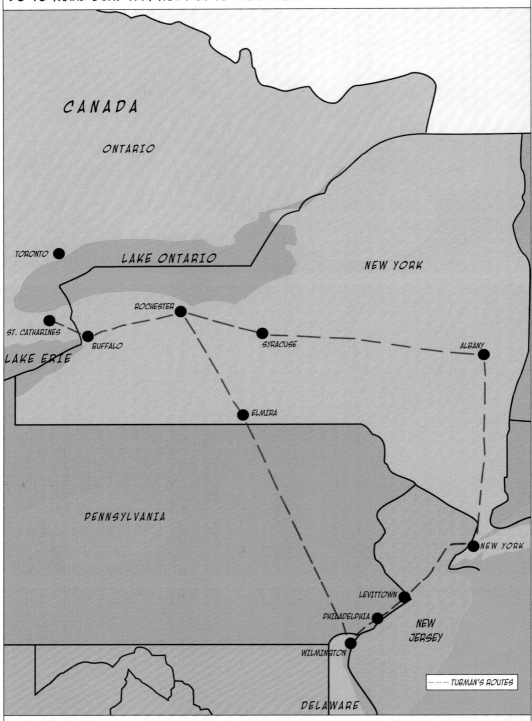

HARRIET TUBMAN AND THE SLAVES SHE HELPED MADE MANY STOPS AS THEY USED THE UNDERGROUND RAILROAD. SOME OF THESE PLACES INCLUDED PHILADELPHIA, ALBANY, ROCHESTER, AND BUFFALO.

SLAVE OWNERS WERE ANGRY THAT THEIR SLAVES WERE RUNNING AWAY.

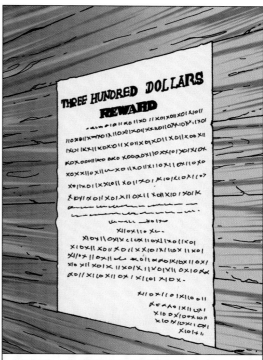

OWNERS OFFERED **REWARDS** FOR THE CAPTURE OF SLAVES OR THE PEOPLE WHO HELPED THEM ESCAPE.

THE TOTAL REWARD FOR TUBMAN'S CAPTURE SOON REACHED $40,000.

YET HARRIET TUBMAN BRAVELY CONTINUED HER WORK. SHE EVEN TRAVELED ON THE TRAIN ONCE. SHE COULD HAVE BEEN SEEN AND CAUGHT.

JOHN BROWN WAS A FAMOUS ABOLITIONIST. HE VISITED ST. CATHARINES TO MEET WITH TUBMAN. BROWN KNEW ALL ABOUT HER WORK.

GENERAL TUBMAN, YOU ARE ONE OF THE BEST AND BRAVEST PEOPLE ON THIS **CONTINENT**.

FOR 10 YEARS, HARRIET TUBMAN SPENT HER TIME AND MONEY RESCUING SLAVES FROM MARYLAND. SHE MADE 19 TRIPS AND HELPED ABOUT 300 PEOPLE TO FREEDOM.

HARRIET TUBMAN WORKED FOR THE UNION ARMY DURING THE CIVIL WAR. MANY OF THE SLAVES SHE FREED BECAME SOLDIERS IN THE UNION ARMY.

AFTER THE WAR, SHE WORKED FOR WOMEN'S RIGHTS. SHE WAS A POPULAR SPEAKER.

HARRIET TUBMAN CONTINUED WORKING FOR THE RIGHTS OF ALL PEOPLE UNTIL SHE DIED IN 1913 AT ABOUT THE AGE OF 91.

THE END

TIMELINE

c. 1822	Araminta Ross is born into slavery in Dorchester County, Maryland.
c. 1828– 1832	Araminta works for a weaver. Araminta catches the measles. Araminta works as a housekeeper and babysitter.
c. 1833	Araminta changes her name to Harriet. Harriet is hurt by an overseer.
c. 1844	Harriet marries freeman John Tubman.
1849	Harriet Tubman's owner, Edward Brodess, dies. Tubman escapes to freedom in Philadelphia. Harriet Tubman meets William Still of the Philadelphia Anti-Slavery Society.
1850	Tubman becomes a conductor on the Underground Railroad. Tubman leads her niece and two children to freedom.
1851	Harriet Tubman returns to Dorchester County to bring John Tubman north. John, who has remarried, does not go with Harriet.
1852– 1860	Tubman continues her work with the Underground Railroad.
1861	Tubman works for the Union army during the Civil War.
1913	Harriet Tubman dies at about the age of 91.

GLOSSARY

abolitionist (a-buh-LIH-shun-ist) A man or woman who worked to end slavery.

betrayed (bih-TRAYD) Turned against.

captured (KAP-churd) Taken control of by force.

Civil War (SIH-vul WOR) The war fought between the Northern and the Southern states of America from 1861 to 1865.

continent (KON-teh-nent) One of Earth's seven large landmasses.

debts (DETS) Things that are owed.

fugitive (FYOO-juh-tiv) Someone who is running away from someone or something.

mission (MIH-shun) A special job or task.

oath (OHTH) A promise.

overseer (OH-ver-see-ur) A person who watches over workers.

plantations (plan-TAY-shunz) Large farms where crops are grown.

rescue (RES-kyoo) To save someone or something.

rewards (rih-WORDZ) Prizes, often of money.

routes (ROOTS) The paths a person takes to get somewhere.

Underground Railroad (UN-dur-grownd RAYL-rohd) A system set up to help slaves move to freedom in the North.

weaver (WEE-ver) Someone who uses thread to make cloth.

INDEX

WEB SITES

Due to the changing nature of Internet links, the Rosen Publishing Group, Inc., has developed an online list of Web sites related to the subject of this book. This site is updated regularly. Please use this link to access the list:
www.powerkidslinks.com/jgb/tubman/